4.50

Jewellery
Unlimited

A selected exhibition of original and
challenging contemporary jewellery
by members of the Association for
Contemporary Jewellery (ACJ)

Organised by the Exhibition
Committee, ACJ-Bristol:
Maike Barteldres, Holly Belsher,
Matt Benton, Inge Braeckevelt,
Jane Eveleigh, Alastair Gill,
Barbie McClure, Tamizan Savill,
Heather Sharrock, Sally Simpson
& Jessica Turrell

www.jewellery-unlimited.org.uk

Catalogue edited by:
Holly Belsher & Jessica Turrell

Published by the ACJ

739·2702 Ba

Jewellery
Unlimited

First published in 2004 by
The Association for Contemporary
Jewellery (ACJ)
P.O.Box 37807 London SW23 1XJ

enquiries@acj.org.uk
www.acj.org.uk

on the occasion of the exhibition
Jewellery-Unlimited
Bristol City Museum and Art Gallery
Bristol BS8 1RL
17 April - 27June 2004

www.jewellery-unlimited.org.uk

Designed by Rodger Martin
and Andy Purnell

Printed by Apple Litho (Bristol) Ltd
Unit 16, Bristol Vale, Hartcliffe Way,
Bristol BS3 5JR

Photographs as credited or
jeweller's own

Model photography by
Mark Simmons
Models:
Ronald Murray, Samantha Parks,
John Rogers, Sarah Braun,
Maria Neath, Ted Braun,
Tom Miles, Anne-Marie Craig

ISBN 0-953 8560-1-1

Cover images from left
Front
Adam Paxon ....brooch
Amanda Doughty ..bangle
Eleanor Barron .....headdress
Nina Osborne ....brooch
Maria Hanson ....object/brooch
Susan May ....bangle
Back
Elizabeth Bone .....bangles
Gill Forsbrook........bangle
Susan Cross ....brooch
Adele Kime............brooch
Jane Moore ....pendant
Jane Adam............bangles

See also Acknowledgements

Jewellery-Unlimited is dedicated to the memory of

Jeremy Rees

1937-2003

who, with Annabel Rees, gave Bristol an early vision of
contemporary studio jewellery with innovative exhibitions
at Arnolfini from 1961 to 1984.

Foreword

Susan Fortune, Chairman of The Association for Contemporary Jewellery

In March 1996 a conference was held at the University of Northumbria in Newcastle. A conference for jewellers organised by jewellers, this was the first of its kind in Britain. There were delegates from 17 countries including members of the Society of North American Goldsmiths (SNAG) and the Forum fur Schmuck, Germany.
If there were some similarities in the structure of the conference to those held annually by SNAG this was not unintentional – there had for some time been a dialogue between many of its members and a significant number of British makers. This had generated respect for SNAG and its achievements.
The conference in Newcastle was inspirational – designers, makers, educationalists, collectors, curators, we were all there. We exchanged ideas, saw great jewellery, and sat up way into the night talking. The final event was a forum to discuss an idea that had been growing for some time in the minds of many UK based jewellers – a British organisation to promote an understanding of contemporary jewellery, to represent the interests of all those involved with contemporary jewellery, and to enable communication between its many enthusiasts. When this was put to the delegates the response was hugely positive and, with some advice from the SNAG and European representatives, the Association for Contemporary Jewellery (ACJ) was born.
The ACJ was finally established in May 1997. Since then, we have held three conferences, in Edinburgh, Birmingham and Manchester. I am the third Chairman in my second year of a three year tenure.
Our membership, which is non-selective and open to all those interested in contemporary jewellery in any capacity, whether amateur or professional, has grown to almost 600 from the UK and abroad. We have been generously supported by the Arts Council of England and, in turn, we support our members in a number of activities. We currently have four Regional Groups through which the Association maintains its regional profile and encourages local activities. Increasingly important is that the Association now has a voice both nationally and internationally and is consulted about issues that affect jewellery, both craft and industry based.

To date most of the Association's activities have been conferences, seminars, and symposia. This has made it possible for members to see the work of well known artists from across the world and to take part in international and national debate throughout the country. But our members too are very successful – in fact almost all the most recent (2000) Jerwood Prize finalists are members – and they exhibit all over the world. Their work is seen in many UK galleries but Jewellery-Unlimited, which has been organised and mounted by ACJ-Bristol, is the first exhibition of work selected from the ACJ membership. It has required months of planning, fundraising and organisation and Bristol is truly lucky that it is their regional group who have had the energy, vision and skill to carry this off with such panache. Jewellery-Unlimited celebrates the diversity and talent that go to make up a unique, exciting and very inclusive group of people as well as the latest trends in an ancient craft.

Susan Fortune
Chairman of The Association for
Contemporary Jewellery

Contemporary Jewellery A Personal Reflection

Professor Dorothy Hogg MBE, Course Leader – Jewellery and Silversmithing, Edinburgh College of Art

Contemporary jewellery cannot be neatly defined. A fascinating richness of diverse approaches has emerged worldwide. I am involved in my own practice and in the education of jewellers and silversmiths at degree level and I can identify the effect of the educational style and post-education support on the character of the work from each country.

Diverse approaches

Our history and traditions affect the nature of education. In British art colleges and universities the educational structure has been based on learning how to make things while also developing as an artist. A student may not know exactly how to make what she imagines, however creativity and a personal vision grow through experimentation and testing of material alongside the acquisition of the necessary skills. Learning through making seems a natural way for individuality to blossom. Development of critical awareness through drawing in all its forms has not lost its importance; this is seen as a key element to the success of the course I lead at Edinburgh College of Art.

After graduation young jewellers have access to start-up and development support through different agencies which also organise selling opportunities, such as New Designers, Chelsea Craft Fair, Goldsmiths Fair and more recently 'Collect' the new art fair for contemporary objects, presented by the Crafts Council, at the V&A. In the UK we have an unsurpassed history of fine metalworking. Over the centuries this has been nurtured by the influence of the Goldsmiths Companies in London and Edinburgh and by the Assay Offices throughout the country. It is no surprise that London is still home to some of the most outstanding traditional craft workshops internationally. Education and other factors in continental Europe produces a subtly different situation. In Germany students are firstly apprenticed to learn skills and only then can they progress to art college to explore the development of their art expression. In Holland the work shown in galleries is generally fine art led. There is a tradition of giving artists a 'stipend' or grant which can be applied for over and over again, allowing jewellers and other artists to develop radical work without the pressure of earning a living. Contemporary jewellery from the Netherlands is strong in wit and inventive in its use of materials. Italians have a historic connection with the use of gold. They do not seem to be hidebound by their roots in the traditional working of it but are prepared to be radical. These differences lead to work which has the stamp of its location

and that shows cultural diversity and richness. It is this diversity that we should celebrate.

Who buys contemporary jewellery?

In the main the purchasers are women who have the confidence to express their character through their choice of jewellery. Economic independence frees them to explore the unconventional through jewellery, with understated clothes as a backdrop.

Generally there is less opportunity or desire to wear traditional, value-based pieces of jewellery as a more casual attitude to clothes and events prevails. Perhaps people are less confident about the security of precious things and may feel less of a target if wearing interestingly designed and conceived contemporary jewellery. Could this be a continuing trend and an opportunity for what we do to be increasingly exposed and appreciated?

In the recent years of financial restriction, galleries have been increasingly reluctant to take risks by showing very innovative work. Many makers respond to this by making more production work and less of the work that might be considered controversial and which does not immediately address the needs of the market place.

How graduates develop

My graduates continue to amaze me – they seem to be endlessly resourceful and adaptable in the development of their careers. Three graduates from 1996 demonstrate this perfectly: one is a designer for Gucci, another is studying for a PhD in Japanese

Metalwork in Tokyo, and the third is new products manager for a large jewellery company in Birmingham. Many others run successful designer maker workshops and exhibit internationally.

Many graduates put together a package of earning activities allowing them to keep on making their work. The packages include among other things: designing for industry part-time, working in a gallery or jewellery business, teaching and lecturing. It impresses me how their career paths remain focused on developing their own work.

Looking back

It is interesting for me to compare the current situation to the time when I graduated. The opportunities for selling work are significantly better than they were in the 1960s. At that time there were only two fledgling galleries in London showing contemporary jewellery, the Ewan Phillips Gallery and Cameo Corner. I was not aware of contemporary jewellery galleries anywhere else in the UK. There were a few technical books but only one on contemporary jewellery, 'Modern Jewellery' by Graham Hughes.

Looking forward

Now in every town of reasonable size in the UK there is a gallery selling individual applied art including jewellery. There is a greater awareness of design in general and the needs of an increasingly informed, educated and affluent public are being catered for by the higher profile that contemporary jewellery has in museums around the world. Books on the subject are numerous and contemporary jewellery is promoted in publications such as Crafts, Metalsmith, Craft Australia and other journals of the applied arts.

Set-up grants, development grants and direct selling through trade fairs and craft fairs are all accessible to individual makers. Via the internet young makers can access information about galleries worldwide and can generate interest internationally by means of personal websites. New possibilities and forms have come from technological advances in cutting and joining metals and other materials. Haptic technology and interactive ways of developing ideas on computer will also lead to new possibilities. Events like 'Collect' will raise the level of quality and inform us all while offering the opportunity to connect with international work and galleries. Now we have the Association for Contemporary Jewellery, started in 1997, which is run by makers and enthusiasts passionate about our subject. We are very fortunate to have members who are prepared to undertake the production of the newsletter 'Findings', the organisation of international conferences and the daunting task of putting on exhibitions such as 'Jewellery-Unlimited'.

I am a great optimist and I know how much better the opportunities are now than in the past. So let us all continue with what we do while trying to find time to experiment and develop, feeding in fresh thinking, encouraging our outlets to work hard for us and to be brave and take risks. Contemporary jewellery in the UK has an approach all of its own, endowed with strength, diversity and character.

Professor Dorothy Hogg MBE
Course Leader –
Jewellery and Silversmithing
Edinburgh College of Art

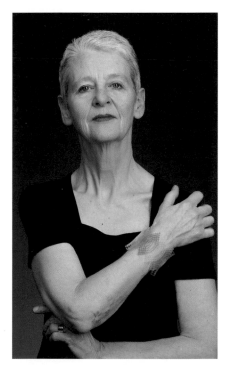

Introduction

Matthew Partington,

Director, National Electronic and Video Archive of the Crafts (NEVAC). Research Fellow, Applied Arts (UWE/V&A)

During the 1963 Royal Variety Performance John Lennon asked, 'will the people in the cheaper seats clap your hands? All the rest of you, if you'll just rattle your jewellery'.[1] Lennon's remark, redolent of the social hierarchies of Britain in the sixties, also reflects a view of jewellery as associated with class, wealth and precious materials. Today's jewellery may still rattle but it is no longer the preserve of the wealthiest classes and the rattling is as likely to be caused by materials such as acrylic and aluminium as silver and gold.

It is a real delight to find an exhibition of contemporary jewellery on this scale in Bristol. Since the early days of the Arnolfini and its association with some of the best new jewellery of the 1960s, 70s and early 80s, Bristol has not hosted a major show of contemporary jewellery. The inclusion in Jewellery-Unlimited of work by internationally renowned makers such as Jane Adam, Maria Hanson, Dorothy Hogg, Jacqueline Mina and Adam Paxon is a testament to the growing reputation of the Association for Contemporary Jewellery as well as a treat for Bristol's jewellery lovers.

One of the aims of the exhibition is 'to promote the area of contemporary studio jewellery to a wide audience, both locally and nationally'[2] and to encourage those who aren't familiar with contemporary studio jewellery to take it seriously, not just as a pretty adornment for the wealthy but as an art form rich in ideas and possibilities and accessible to everyone. The dictionary definition of jewellery as 'personal ornaments, such as

necklaces, rings, or bracelets, that are made from or contain jewels and precious metals'[3] is perhaps how many people think of jewellery. Whilst this is true of much of what can be bought on the high street, contemporary studio jewellery of the sort found in Jewellery-Unlimited is a much more complex and thought-provoking area for study.

Whereas function is still a central concern, studio jewellery now encompasses performance and conceptual art and its boundaries are no longer fixed to the 'must haves' of precious metals and jewels. Materials range from the expected – gold, silver and platinum to the less common – wool, lycra, concrete, eggshells and chicken bones. Whilst those unfamiliar with the range of studio jewellery now being made may be surprised by the diversity of materials and forms on display, the power of this exhibition is to be found in the accessibility of the jewellery both in terms of its cost and wearability.

Since the great blossoming of studio jewellery of the 1970s it is no longer seen simply as a decorative art but as an art form rich in ideas which frequently engages with architecture, fine art and a whole range of other craft media. Traditional jewellery forms such as necklaces, earrings, brooches, rings and bracelets predominate, but there is also engagement with technology, not least in the form of the light emitting diodes (LEDs) used in Ulli Oberlack's work. She describes how she aims to, 'exploit the intrinsic characteristics of light on the body creating new forms of adornment'.[4] Currently engaged in practice-based PhD research at Central St Martins College in London, Ulli represents a new breed of jeweller – confident with new technology and post-graduate research methodologies. Stephen Bottomley, another jeweller embracing new technologies, interweaves CAD/CAM[5] with handcraft. Whilst the vast majority of studio jewellery is designed and made by hand, Bottomley's Orbit ring and Debut Pendant/Ring are designed 'with' a computer and manufactured by a computer controlled machine before the final finishing by hand. His necklaces are designed with computer software that creates the transferable designs and patterns for the metal. This is jewellery literally at the cutting edge of technology.

Bottomley and Oberlack are engaging with technology whilst others are looking to contemporary culture for their influences. Katherine Bailey's witty "Bling, Bling", a large 'nugget' of gold-plate teetering atop a ring reflects youth culture and issues of consumption. Tina Lilienthal's necklaces based on the seven deadly sins reflect an interest in subverting jewellery mores through the mixture of cheap and expensive materials and oversized and unconventional imagery. Jivan Astfalck's pieces are woven around historical and personal narratives and include bones, photographs and fabric as well as precious metals. Her interest in how 'ideas of femininity' are 'mythologised in our culture' gives her work a conceptual slant which is not reliant on technique and materials for its impact but asks us to look beyond the materials to the ideas implicit in the jewellery.
Jung-Ji Kim's exquisite neckpieces are triumphs of making skill and composition: 'One of my prime considerations in using precious materials is to present them in unexpected ways while retaining all their beauty and achieving

comfort and wearability for the client. I attempt to make flexible constructions that lend themselves to the human form. I love the idea that the work interacts with the body and its movement, generating a vitality sometimes lost by its static display on a shelf'.[6]
Jung-Ji's description of her approach reflects what many of the makers in this exhibition say about their work – that they aim for a balanced relationship between the jewellery

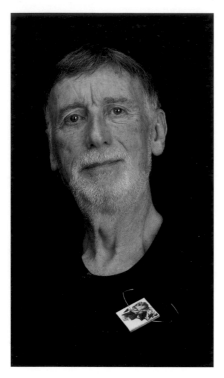

exhibitions that the viewer is catered for but the maker and wearer are usually left out of the picture. The jewellery is displayed on stands in cases and the fact that they were made by hand to be worn by a real person is assumed rather than acknowledged in the display.
The inclusion in the gallery of Mark Simmonds' elegant photographs of the jewellery being worn helps restore the balance and bring the exhibition to life. A further contextual aid is found in the cases containing jewellery making tools and explanations of techniques and processes. These visual aids and the range of approaches and styles on display help to make Jewellery Unlimited a welcoming and visually stimulating exhibition.
I am sure that the gallery will resound to the sound of visitor's jewellery being rattled in appreciation of the work on display.

and the wearer. Jewellery, by its very nature as a media made to be worn, has retained its function. Whereas many contemporary craft objects are made to be admired on a plinth or shelf, jewellery's primary function is still as an adornment to the human form. This show is a celebration of that function and all of the work on display can and should be worn for it to be fully appreciated.
It is a common problem with jewellery

Matthew Partington
Director, National Electronic and
Video Archive of the Crafts (NEVAC)
Research Fellow, Applied Arts
(UWE/V&A)
www.media.uwe.ac.uk/nevac

[1] Oxford Dictionary of Twentieth Century Quotations, 1998, p.187.
[2] www.acj.org.uk/jsp/pages/events – web-site of the Association for Contemporary Jewellery.
[3] Concise Oxford English Dictionary, 2002.
[4] www.csm.linst.ac.uk/displaynews.asp – web-site of Central St Martins College of Art and Design.
[5] CAD/CAM - computer aided design/computer aided manufacture.
[6] www.caa.org.uk/cvs/kim_jung-ji.htm – web-site of Contemporary Applied Arts, London.

Jewellery
Unlimited

The work displayed in the exhibition was chosen from submitted slides and disc images by an invited selection panel. The selectors were asked to choose work that they considered to be jewellery at its most bold and innovative in terms of design, concept, materials and technique.

THE SELECTION PANEL

Cynthia Cousens is a jeweller who has exhibited nationally and internationally. She was shortlisted for the Jerwood prize in 2000. Cynthia's work is held in a number of major public collections including the V&A, National Museums of Scotland and the Crafts Council.

Sarah James is a former Craft Development Officer. She is the owner of Made, Contemporary Craft and Interiors Gallery based in Bristol. Sarah was a selector for Chelsea Craft Fair in 2003.

Elizabeth Turrell is Senior Fellow in Enamel at the University of the West of England, and a practicing artist who exhibits internationally. She is also a director of Studio Fusion Gallery, Oxo Tower Wharf, London.

Karin Walton is the Curator of Applied Art at Bristol City Museum and Art Gallery.

If you wish to make contact with an individual exhibitor please address your enquiries to:

The Administrator, The Association for Contemporary Jewellery (ACJ) P.O.Box 37807, London SW23 1XJ

e-mail: enquiries@acj.org.uk

The Jewellers

Jane Adam

A piece of jewellery creates unique
physical and symbolic, visual and
tactile relationships with its owner,
with its maker and perhaps with the
people who see it being worn.
It can change or enhance the way
the wearer feels about herself and
how she appears to others.

91 Triangle Drops Neckpiece
– dyed anodised aluminium,
stainless steel, silver.

Bangles – anodised, dyed &
textured aluminium

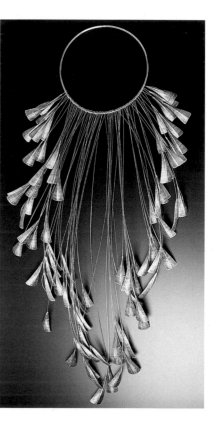

JOËL DEGEN

16

Marianne Anderson

Ornament and Order.
Studying the context of traditional ornamentation within the decorative arts highlights its beauty, meaning and importance. The arrangement of repeated parts into patterns creates symmetries and contrasts which are alluring and elegant, and fulfil the basic human desire to embellish. In my jewellery, pierced silhouettes of oxidised silver are systematically arranged and intersected by grids of gemstones and pearls, or scattered randomly to deconstruct controlled patterns, creating bold fragmented images on an intricate scale. Layering motifs, patterns and theories embedded in ornaments history decodes certain rules of decoration, presenting contemporary ornament of a detailed and wearable nature.

Ornament & Order series Brooches
– oxidised silver, glass

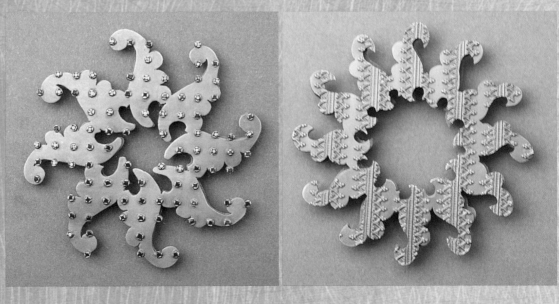

17

Hidemi Asano

My work combines the primary process of European jewellery technique with the aesthetic of the Japanese tradition of minimalism. I create sculptural forms using both precious and non-precious materials with my own recipe of powdered stone and resin. I make natural pebbles that are held secure with silver or gold. In 'Branch' the metal is formed to echo the growth patterns and strength that is present in nature. 'Sara Sara' is a Japanese expression to describe water flowing in a river or how the tip of the calligraphy brush moves. The philosophy behind this, which is also my theme, is tranquil movement and the serene moment.

Sara Sara Neckpiece – silver, resin
Branch Pendants – silver resin
Branch Earrings – 18ct yellow gold, resin, diamond

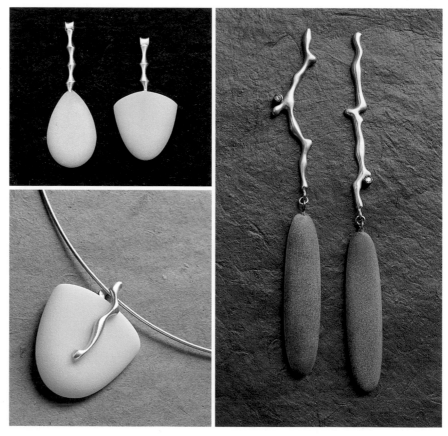

Jivan Astfalck

I am interested in the hidden undercurrents of subjective narratives, which in my view we all invest in objects. The stories I tell in my work are a mixture of historical and autobiographical material, fiction, fairy tales and critical theory. In all our experience in the world of action there is a general need for personalising what is alien to us in order to understand it, even if this understanding is ultimately recognised as an illusion. Stories, signs and symbols are thus appropriated as a process of assimilation. For some time now I have been mainly preoccupied with devotional objects, constructions around ideas of femininity and how these are mythologised in our culture.

On Memory and Loss,
Neckpiece – silver, chicken
bones, fine gold, pearls

Bandages for Broken Hearts
– mixed media, fabricated

Kathleen Bailey

My work is influenced by a preoccupation with traditional jewellery, with aspects such as fastenings and packaging. A desire to rework or find an alternative method for securing a piece to the body, or allowing the notion of how a piece is stored or packed away to influence its design.

These things are at the back of my mind as I observe the mechanics and qualities of everyday materials and objects, and I will always be considering how I can apply these particular concepts to my jewellery.

Bling Bling, Ring
– copper, silver, gold plate

Demerara Ring
– sugar crystal, silver

Engineered Earrings
– silver, ribbon

JOËL DEGEN

PETE MCCAUSLAND

Eleanor Barron

Eleanor Barron graduated from Glasgow School of Art in 1998, she specialises in creating jewellery and hair ornaments that combine precious metals with non-precious materials such as feathers, porcupine quills and beads. The use of different materials lends the jewellery a delicate quality and gives a feeling of movement to each piece.

Red Spiral Headdress
– silver, red feathers

White Fairy Crown
– silver, white feathers

Harriet Bedford

Harriet Bedford graduated from Plymouth College of Art and Design in 2002 and since then has been working on a series of pierced metal collections inspired by the art nouveau movement and botanical structures and forms. There is a certain quirky individuality to each piece due to asymmetry or the way it moves or lies against the body.

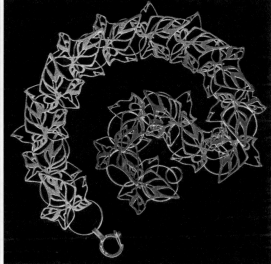

Anemone Necklace –
pierced silver chain

Ivy Necklace –
pierced silver chain

Holly Belsher

Sticks and Stones: I love the British landscape. Walking in a wood or on a beach, I pick up tiny bits and pieces of debris. A twig with fascinating leaf scars, or a perfect oval white quartz pebble from a Suffolk shingle beach.

By casting twigs in gold and silver I make them into precious objects. By pinning a carefully selected stone to them I ask the viewer to appreciate its subtle shape and colour and to really see what is usually disregarded as natural litter, trodden unnoticed underfoot.

JOËL DEGEN

Sticks & Stones Necklace – cast silver, natural pebble, 18ct gold bead

Sticks & Stones Brooch – cast silver, white quartz, Suffolk pebble

Sticks & Stones Brooch – cast silver & 18ct gold, yellow quartz pebble

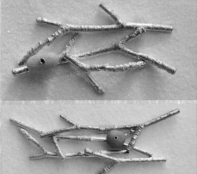

23

Matt Benton

Fibre reinforced resin is typically used in hi-tech industrial applications. Its useful properties include a high strength to weight ratio and its ability to be cast or moulded. I was interested in researching a low-tech method of manufacture and the inclusion of colour. These brooches are the results of my experiments. They are made from different types of material soaked in clear setting epoxy resin, laminated under pressure. The cut-out shapes give a clue to the domestic use of the material each brooch is made from.

Glass Cloth Brooch
– laminated tea towel fabric, resin

All Purpose Cloth Brooch
– laminated All Purpose cloth, resin

Duster Brooch
– laminated fabric, resin

Roberta Bernabei

My work responds to the human body and uses its surrounding spaces as a parameter of measurement in objects, which enable wearers and observers to understand and reconsider the confines of their bodies and the external world. A process of subtraction from the traditional setting prompted the discovery of intriguing 'memory spaces'.

My transparent silicone objects encase 'memories of cast space' and oscillate between presence and imperceptibility, as delicacies of form are revealed by the interplay between light and shadow. The microcosm is transformed into the macrocosm by magnifying the nuances of the body's spaces in lens-like forms.

Necklace
– painted brass, silicone
Ring – silver, silicone
Brooch
– painted brass, silicone

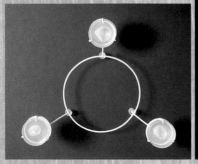

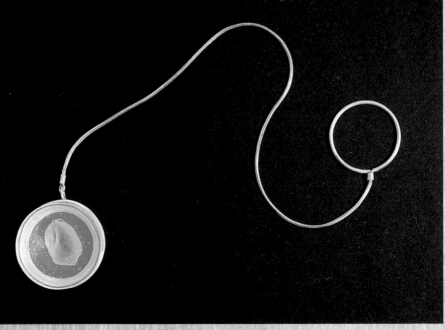

Kelvin Birk

Some of my inspiration is taken from modern architecture.

Part of my present work could be compared to architectural details, partly because of the choice of the materials used, partly because of the essential and pure design.

I design and produce jewellery as well as larger objects and silverware, often using uncommon materials in combination with precious metals. My project, 'Silver and Concrete', is a challenge to the common perception and image of these two materials. I try to question the existing notion of 'value' by treating concrete like a precious material.

Conical Brooches – silver
Conical Rings – silver, gold plating

Petra Bishai

The spines of the creeping devil cactus form an array of starbursts – the key to the plant's survival is attraction and defence. Decoration becomes function – the plant adapts to its environment using pattern and colour as lures whilst creating a barrier through the use of sharp spines.

Petra looks at the concept of attraction and defence whilst living in a large city, the jewellery is a response to questions of adaptation and interaction. Her jewellery is designed to stimulate attention, attract the daring and allow interaction within the environment. Light, subtle and elegant, enjoyable to wear, it invites comment and works well with the body.

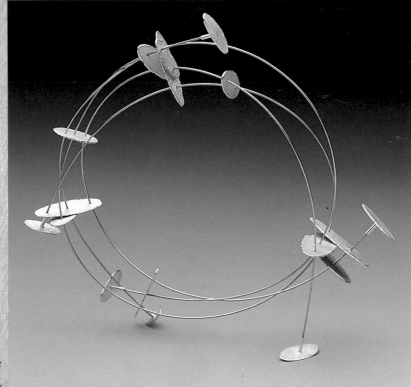

*Water Lily Bracelet
– stainless steel,
fine silver, 18ct gold*

*Water Lily Neckpiece
– stainless steel,
fine silver, 18ct gold*

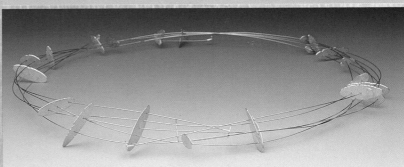

Elizabeth Bone

Material and process guided by order, balance and a modernist influence form the basis for my work. Clean lines, geometric forms, honesty in the use of materials. My working vocabulary contains many visual references to mechanical production, though this belies the fact that the pieces are produced entirely by hand processes: sawing, filing, shaping and coaxing, striving for precision and purity. This is what motivates me.

Moon Ring – silver
Bangles – silver
Growth Ring Brooch
– silver, gold plate

JOËL DEGEN

28

Stephen Bottomley

Stephen Bottomley divides his time between his Brighton studio and lecturing work at the University of Brighton and Hastings College of Art.

His jewellery typically explores low relief texture, pattern and form drawn from computer aided design, photography and harmonics. These textural surfaces are applied to plain and coloured silver and gold, juxtapose with simple rhythmic shapes that express clarity of form and structure.

The result integrates contemporary tools of perception – like computer design software, microscopic images and digital photography – with the traditional and evolving tools of the goldsmith.

Debut Pendant/Ring – CAD/CAM Rapid prototype form, silver

Silk Ruff Necklace – silver, stainless steel, pearls

Arcs Necklace – silver, rubber, stainless steel, pearls

Orbit Ring – CAD/CAM Rapid prototype form, silver

Sarah Braun

Because of my professional background in making large-scale textiles, I find the challenge of creating jewellery – centimetres rather than metres – very exciting. Combining recycled materials with more traditional ones into something playful has allowed me to exploit my interest in kinetic art as the jumping-off point for movable pieces.

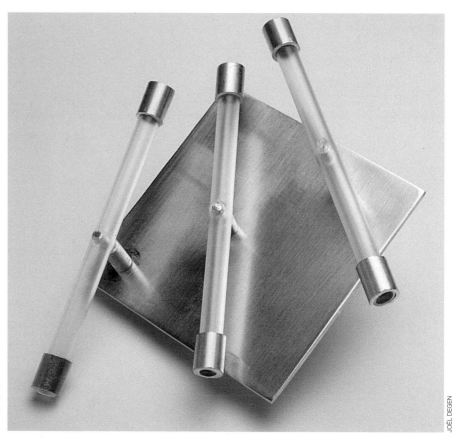

Movable Piece, Brooch – silver, plastic acupuncture needle covers

JOEL DEGEN

Michael Carberry

My aim is to create work that reflects the process of its construction, allowing the surface qualities produced to trace their own development. Hammer and file marks are not removed, so creating a visual reference to illustrate the techniques and physical properties of my work. This intuitive approach to manipulating metal helps to capture a feeling of spontaneity and freshness contained within the resulting artefacts. The pieces look as if they have grown from the metal, they are hammered and forged into strong bold sculptured forms that capture the force and energy involved in the process.

Repetition – series of fine silver forged rings

Shimara Carlow

While studying at Glasgow School of Art, I experimented with hand-made paper and silver as media for creating large sculptural jewellery. My work has always been very tactile and organic and the use of paper enhances this tactility and also brings a light translucent quality to the jewellery.

During my year at Bishopsland Workshops I have developed a range of silver jewellery which continues the tactile theme, with small silver pods assembled to hang freely from neckpieces, bracelets and earrings. Recent developments to this range incorporate small paper forms, which hang alongside silver pods, creating a contrast in material and incorporating sound and movement into the work.

White Honesty Bangle
– white honesty, silk, silver

Lin Cheung

As a young girl, cosmetics were forbidden. I grew up coveting not the desirability of cosmetics to look beautiful, but for the beauty of the objects themselves.

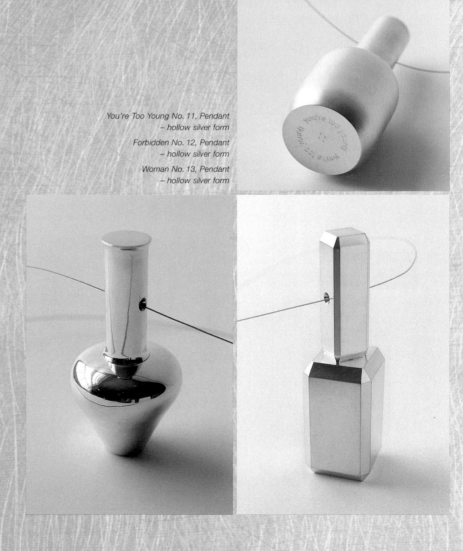

You're Too Young No. 11, Pendant
– hollow silver form
Forbidden No. 12, Pendant
– hollow silver form
Woman No. 13, Pendant
– hollow silver form

Barbara Christie

My inspiration is found within the organised geometry of architectural spaces. My need to reorganise so many ideas exercises me in all ways. Although I am a gregarious human being I am a reclusive and introverted maker.

If I were to make more than three pieces of jewellery in a narrative series, I would lose my sense of humour. I know when to stop.

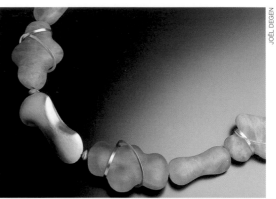

Necklace – 18ct gold, aquamarine

Rings – silver, chrysoprase and aquamarine

JOËL DEGEN

Yvonne Coffey

Connections and intimacy are preoccupations of Yvonne Coffey's work. She draws on her skill as a glass maker and jeweller to explore the intriguing dynamics in personal relationships. Traditional techniques are applied to a range of materials, developing subtle and tactile qualities in the pieces.

These necklaces are designed to be worn and enjoyed individually as well as relating to the work's underlying 'story'. As a result each piece is part of an overall themed structure but seen or worn individually has its own inherent tale to tell. Overall Yvonne's work is a glance at the relationships we all have and need.

Male II Necklace
– cut lead crystal, hematite

Female II Necklace
– gold plated silver, moonstones

Male IV Necklace
– cut lead crystal, hematite

JOËL DEGEN

35

Alan Craxford

All the work I produce is one-off and is hand engraved and carved. This is a concentrated, focused activity as metal once removed cannot be replaced. Each piece has a significance as part of my own inner process, fundamental to which is the need to produce something exquisite.

One aims to continually refine imagery, technique and materials to give expression to what is in one's deepest unconscious self, always aspiring to produce the finest and most beautiful work.

Mandala Brooch – diamond spiral, oxidised silver, 18ct white gold, diamonds

JOËL DEGEN

Susan Cross

I work primarily in precious metals, creating rhythmic forms of line and texture that explore the interface between constructed textiles and jewellery. Using techniques such as wrapping, binding and coiling, ideas for jewellery pieces are interwoven and evolve, often as a direct result of the making process. The integration and exposure of the technique has become a significant artistic and design element in the work that I make.

Recent travels to the east, India and Japan, have inspired the use of materials such as spun paper cord and thread. The introduction of colour through non-precious materials promotes spontaneity and a freshness of approach.

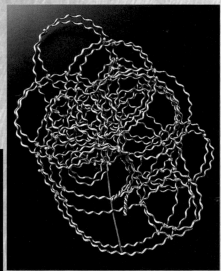

Loop Brooch
– oxidised silver, Crystaline

Crimped Loop Brooch
– oxidised silver, 18ct gold

Chroma Brooch
– oxidised silver, Crystaline

JOËL DEGEN

Amanda Doughty

My jewellery is made primarily in silver and gold, I often use diamonds to enhance and accentuate the edges of the metal forms. I am also interested in the precious nature of diamonds and like to explore concealing small stones within my work. The wearer knows that they are contained within the piece but they are not always visible. I combine simple, bold, geometric elements subtly contrasting the colours of the metals with complementary semi-matt, brushed and shiny finishes. Inspired by my photography of simple, repetitive, mostly man-made features in the landscape, the forms in my jewellery are refined through experimenting with geometric sections, materials and forms at my workbench.

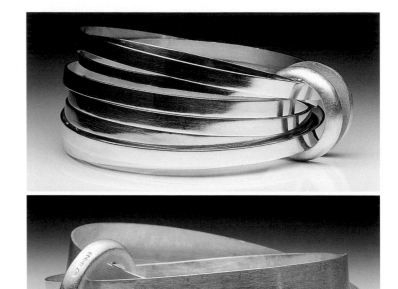

Multiple Bangle – silver with double element

Bangle – 18ct gold & silver (Bi-metal) with silver and 18ct element

Earrings – 18ct gold, some with diamonds

Anne Earls-Boylan

My recent work explores the relationship between cultural heritage, materials and maker. Within this context I use a mixture of media, humble threads, old linen, wood veneer ebony, precious metals and contemporary reflective materials. For me, materials have a resonance which can evoke the past or look forward to the future.

By using fabrics and threads I consciously want to address the historical role of women in my culture. In Keep-Safe 1&2 (my most recent work) the reflective material mixed with 22ct gold symbolises thoughts about motherhood and the complex feelings surrounding growing up during the troubles when life seemed so precious yet transient.

JOEL DEGEN

Brooch "Keep Safe"
– 22ct gold, formed
reflective material

Collar "Keep Safe"
– 22ct gold, formed
reflective material

Diana East

The thinking behind these pieces is based on a continuing investigation into the nuts and bolts of identity and consciousness. 'Reaction' and 'Loop' refer in my imagination to the movement of positive ions in the tissues of the brain.

I am aware that there is a strange loop here because I am trying to visualise the very process that I am using for visualisation.

Reaction, Neckpiece – flame worked glass and stainless steel

Loop – flame worked glass, copper and stainless steel

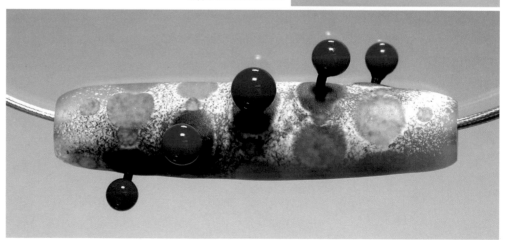

Emma Farquharson

My work is currently undergoing a focused and in-depth elaboration that explores the process of wrapping lengths of silver and gold wire, with hollow tubing to form bracelets, cuffs and bangles. I refer intuitively to the spiral conformation of a nautilus shell and the endless spiralling of a cylindrical helix. I love the technical process of making, allowing the materials to direct the work. The designs evolve out of the process of making, forming something, taking it apart and then putting it back together in a new way. I would describe my work as a synthesis of design process, material and technique.

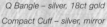

Q Bangle – silver, 18ct gold
Compact Cuff – silver, mirror

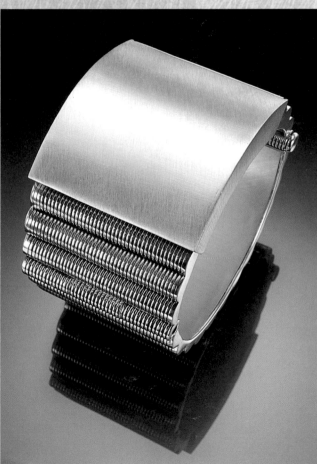

41

Gail Ferriman

'Political Gems' started from a
light-hearted response to the
'Monica Lewinsky and Bill Clinton'
affair. Visual puns and text from
newspapers were used to create a
collection for the Clothes Show in
Birmingham at the time.
The work has rolled on to include
other newsworthy events and
more recently recording thoughts
on the Euro.

*Holding Folding Brooch
– anodised aluminium,
surgical steel*

*Bill and Monica Cigar Brooch
– anodised aluminium, silver*

*Holding Folding Studs
– anodised aluminium,
surgical steel*

Anne Finlay

Geometric themes and non-precious materials are at the core of my work. I design by experimenting with materials and exploring construction, composition and colour. In the process I try to combine components, such as sheet material, cable, tube and wire in innovative ways, as well as integrating decorative and functional elements. My objectives are simplicity, elegance and structural order.

Necklace – acrylic, stainless steel

Brooch – laminate, slate, stainless steel, acrylic, nylon

Brooch – stainless steel, acrylic, nylon

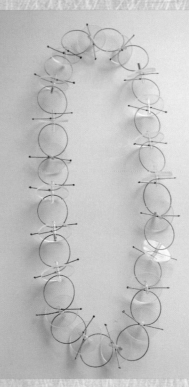

Shelby Ferris Fitzpatrick

All work focuses on concepts and structure. This includes unusual rings with silk or moving elements, multi-functional work with innovative mechanisms or fittings or shapes, musical elements inside metal structures, units which unscrew or turn, rings which float on the hand, collections of silk/silver jewellery, kinetic work and 'off the body' necklaces.

Off the Body, Necklace
– silver, silk and plastic

Off the Body, Necklace
– silver, crystal

MIKE BUSSETT

STEPHEN BRAYNE

Gill Forsbrook

My jewellery is made from plastics and metals, plastics being the predominant material. I use several different types of plastic in my work including polypropylene, polycarbonate, PVC and acrylic. Qualities of materials which interest me are colour, translucency, transparency and reflection. I aim to exploit these qualities in my jewellery.

Bangle – Polypropylene, PVC, aluminium, silver

Bangle – Polypropylene, aluminium, silver

Bangle – Polypropylene, Polycarbonate, PVC, aluminium, silver

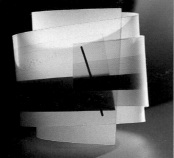

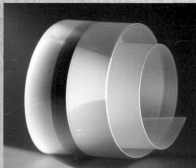

45

Alastair Gill

Resulting from my architectural
background and interest my work is
an ongoing essay on the
exploration of space. How it is
defined, how it progresses from
one part to another, how it
stimulates our imagination.

Reflections, Brooch – silver, 18ct gold

Twist, Earrings – silver

JAN BLAKE

Jan Goodey

This work refers to both the journey and the static area on which traces of travelling remain. The land holds traces of every journey it has played host to, changed slightly by each one. The tiny nomadic beads move along their paths in response to the movements of the wearer. In some sense it is also, inevitably, a metaphor for a more personal journey – the road less travelled. The process of making work is exploratory and never quite arrives, there is always another direction to take, a new path to follow. The path is continuous, the destinations different.

The Road to Nowhere, Necklace – silver, steel and turquoise

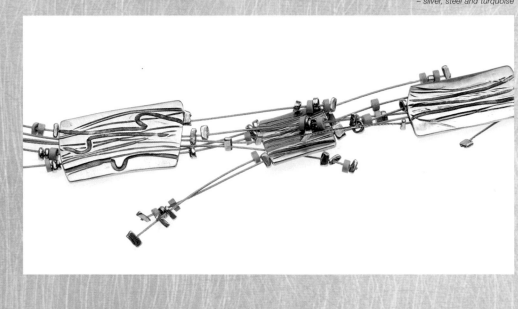

Jo Haines

Through our repeated visual experiences of everything around us we learn to perceive quickly and automatically. If things are too complicated or contrastingly too boring, we ignore them.

We try to find something recognisable in everything we see and in doing so see what we want to see rather than what actually exists. Intentionally hindering perception can make it active and interesting. Through making familiar things seem unfamiliar I am trying to force thought and questioning in the viewer, through your process of recognition and what is being suggested, rather than providing the opportunity for an automatic understanding.

Long Brooch with Faces
– resin, acrylic

Square Brooch with Faces
– resin, acrylic

Square Brooch with Faces
– resin, acrylic

Maria Hanson

There is a sensuous pleasure to be derived from geometry, which the human eye reacts to positively. This pleasure is particularly evident in response to the circle, there is a beauty and harmony in the infinite continuous quality of the unbroken line. The visual language used within these objects/jewels makes reference to mathematics but balances both analytical and instinctive judgement. Although construction is primarily in precious metals, the combining of elements such as nylon mono-filament enables colour and tactility to be explored, and encourages the audience to question the intrinsic value of materials within the context of jewellery.

Sun # 3,4,5 Brooches
– silver, nylon filaments

Sun # 3, Object/Brooch
– silver, nylon filaments, acetal

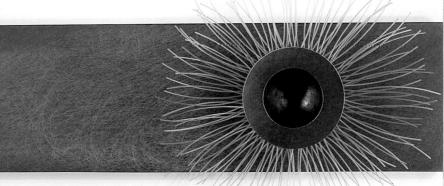

Zoë Harding

The designs for these pieces have been inspired by microscopic imagery of cells and cell structures found in the human body. At high levels of magnification, these cell structures are complex and fascinating. In these images I look for a way to translate them into jewellery. Typically I draw and edit images on computer to realise a design and produce striking, contemporary and unique pieces of jewellery using precious metals, sometimes incorporating gemstones and other natural materials such as vintage coral.

Neuron Neckpiece
– silver, coral, precious stones

Square Coral Ring
– silver, coral

Loekie Heintzberger

Loekie Heintzberger's work creates a world in which she combines innovative ideas with designs of the purest simplicity. Her collections include a variety of uniquely crafted individual pieces and small production lines. This ranges from large silver objects to fine jewellery. Gold is the main material used in her jewellery. She incorporates elements of elegance, movement and flexibility often combining precious and unconventional materials, making her work unique.

Wrap Necklaces – 18ct yellow gold

Ashley Heminway

I want to produce jewellery that can be experienced even when it cannot be possessed, something that has an impact on both the wearer and the viewer. I feel my jewellery should suggest the sexuality of the wearer by its shape, colour and positioning on the body.

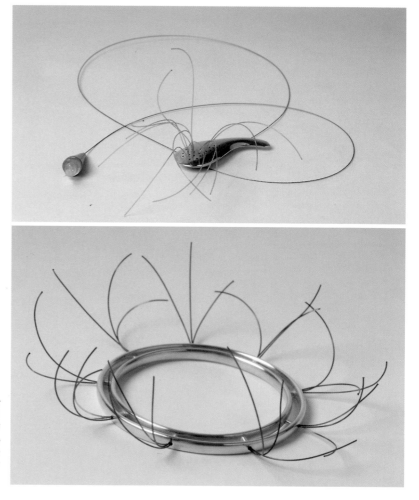

*Medusa, Pendant
– hollow form silver,
nylon attachments*

*Passion Bangle
– silver with nylon
attachments*

Catherine Hills

My jewellery is inspired by natural forms and unites sensuous smooth shapes with highly textured surfaces. The creative process excites and stimulates me to produce work which is a sensitive response to the demand for distinctive, affordable jewellery. Filling the client's needs is critical and attention to detail ensures excellence in a piece that looks and feels right. My production range maximises the use of colour, texture and form. It is innovative in that it uses interchangeable components and subtle surface treatments warranting countless possibilities. The one-off pieces have a dialogue with the production work resulting in a dynamic and complementary relationship.

Genesis Neckpiece
– silver, oxidised silver, 18ct gold

Catkin Cluster Star Necklace
– silver, oxidised silver

Janet Hinchliffe McCutcheon

I am always attempting to remove unnecessary detail; the simplification of a piece is a continuous process. There is a personal preference for certain shapes and forms and when they are worked upon they become your own. The pieces of jewellery must be enjoyed by the wearer and noticed by the observer. Necklaces can be rearranged and worn in different ways and one can fiddle with the detail of moving parts. The materials also invite one to touch.

Square Rings – silver with oxidised silver detail & gold

Dorothy Hogg

My aesthetic is driven by my subconscious mind and reflects in an abstract way events and changes in my life. The structure of the way it moves and symbolic thoughts around this preoccupy my design process. I work mainly in precious metal and am fascinated by the way forms can be constructed in metal to be solid looking but are in reality hollow. These forms are not heavy but light and contain space. I make tube which is generally oval in section and of various dimensions. I use the colour red for its symbolic value. Parallel to making jewellery I have been involved in education and have taught and assessed at various art institutions since 1972. For almost twenty years now I have been lucky enough to be Head of the Jewellery and Silversmithing Department at Edinburgh College of Art. I am committed to ensuring that the progression from college to the professional world is more accessible to current students than it was to those of my generation.

Artery Series Neckpiece – silver, felt
Artery Series Brooches – silver, felt

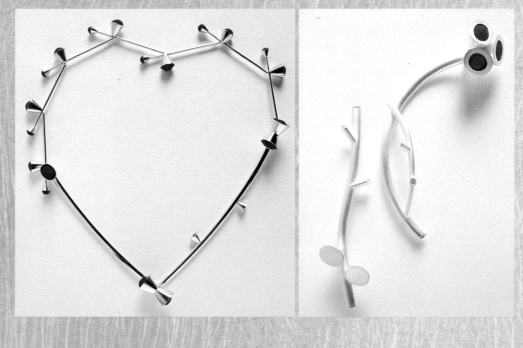

Ulla Hörnfeldt

Gemstones with strong shapes and
unusual markings are the starting
point for my jewellery.
Inspiration for my work comes from
various sources ranging from
architecture to natural objects.
The finished pieces have a clean
and sculpted quality.

*Pendant – silver, rock
crystal, chlorophyte*

Yoko Izawa

When immersed in creative activities I feel that the sense of beauty and value within my culture surfaces and moulds my work. For my means of expression I feel more comfortable when the work has a quality of ambiguity or transience. My interest for some time has been in containing, covering or wrapping things. The search has been for something illusive. The function and material nature of jewellery does not concern me as much as the presence and feeling of an object. These pieces reflect my assumption that although certainty is often required in modern society, ambiguous expression has been the most distinctive characteristic found in Japanese values and religious beliefs.

Veiled ring 1 – Lycra, nylon, silver, 18ct, perspex

Veiled ring 2 – Lycra, nylon, silver, 18ct, perspex

Veiled ring 3 – Lycra, nylon, silver, 18ct, perspex

Veiled Jewelley 2 – Lycra, nylon, silver

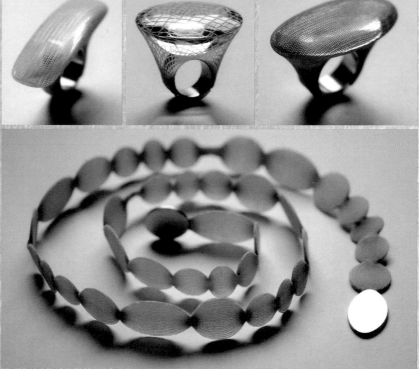

Nuala Jamison

"Plastic it's fantastic
Don't break it
Man-made chemicals –
any way you like it."

Levi Tafari

*Petal Necklace
– silver, acrylic*

*Petal Bracelet
– silver, acrylic*

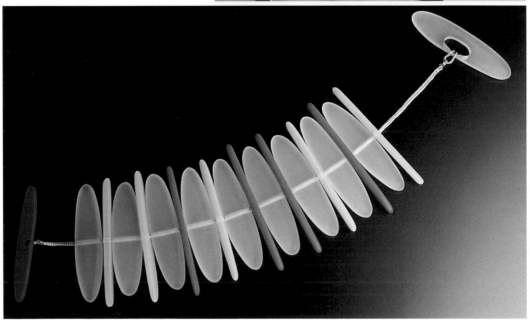

Jasmin Karger

I mainly use emery scratched silver
for my work because I like this
rough look combined with
burnished edges or polished parts.
Some of my pieces are meant to be
little objects with a playful inside.

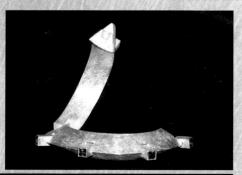

Bracelet
– silver, swarogem stones

Sarah Keay

My work is primarily based on the forms that can be found in nature, especially those that derive from the sea and sea creatures.
The pieces involve numerous experiments with various colours, textures and forms and the use of non-traditional materials.

Bubblegum, Neckpiece – french knitting, rubber, wire, fine silver

Ruby Ring – knitting, wire, found materials

Sea Pod Neckpiece – knitting, wire, found materials

Sarah Kettley

My research concerns the positive role that craft may play in the creation of novel personal technology products. These pieces are beginning to explore the natural environment, in particular land, sea and skyscapes, to inform a familiar aesthetic for the technology-shy. These will form the basis of a range of computational products that are design- rather than technology-led, and which allow their wearers a range of self-expression.

East Coast, Brooch – silver, 18ct gold, Formica, pigment

Sky, Brooch – 18ct red/yellow golds

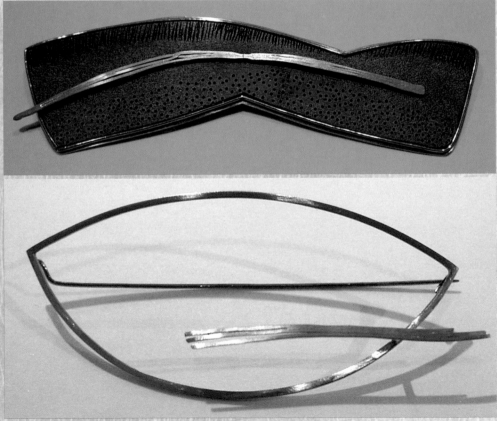

Jung-Ji Kim

To me, jewellery is something between sculpture and garment. My pieces are functional, as they are intended for bodily adornment, yet they may also be seen as sculptural pieces in which spatial relations between mass and void or linear and solid are exactingly constructed.

One of my prime considerations in using precious materials is to present them in unexpected ways while retaining all of their beauty, and achieving comfort and wearability for the client. I attempt to make flexible constructions that lend themselves to the human form. I love the idea that the work interacts with the body and its movement, generating a vitality sometimes lost by static display on a shelf.

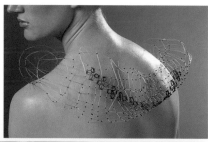

Flower Pattern Neckpiece
– silver, 18ct gold, nylon
Neckpiece – silver, 18ct gold

Adele Kime

My work is inspired by nature's way of encasing and protecting. I create sensuous forms which, when worn, will invite intrigue and speculation around their construction.

A fragility is perceived yet in reality there is a self-supporting strength in structure. I have developed a unique technique creating sculptural pieces by hand wrapping coloured threads into 3D see-through, hardened structures integrated with precious metals. Like mini sculptures they adorn the body, perhaps moving with it or accentuating a part of it in a dramatic and decorative way.

Loop Brooch
– silver and thread fibres

Pitcher Brooch
– silver and 9ct gold, thread fibres

Pod Neckpiece
– silver and thread fibres

63

Sarah King

'Light Constructions' was a solo
exhibition at Arai Atelier Gallery,
Tokyo in summer 2003. This
marked the beginning of a new
body of work exploring
construction, spaces, absence,
lightness, surfaces and subtle
differences.

All pieces are white and transparent
resin or silver. The group is limited
to rings and bangles to focus on
their sculptural and relative qualities.

Light Construction 3, Bangle
– resin & jesmonite

Light Construction 4, Bangle – resin

Light Construction 5 & 6,
Bangle and Ring – resin, silver

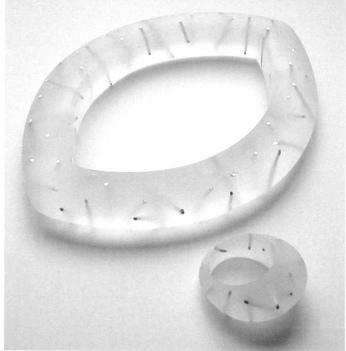

Daphne Krinos

These pieces are designed around the stones they contain. I often buy them because of their odd shape or cut and I try to make a metal object to hold them and make them the centre of attention. Sometimes colours reflect personal moods and experiences, the presence or lack of light where I live.

Andrew Lamb

My jewellery is inspired by linear pattern, repeating lines and natural forms. I use fine lengths of gold, platinum and silver wire, layered twisted and overlapping to make delicately shaped pieces. I "play" with the wires, combining different materials to create subtle colour shifts and twisting various sections to generate rippling textures.

I love working in an experimental way and endeavour to explore all possibilities; changing scale, trying new shapes, using different quantities and lengths of wire, always ready for a new challenge. Through layering wires in three dimensional forms I like to create jewellery which also has an added dimension by demonstrating moiré effects.

Optical Earrings – platinum, 18ct yellow gold wire

Optical Necklace – 18ct yellow gold wire

Brooches – 18ct yellow/ white/red gold wire

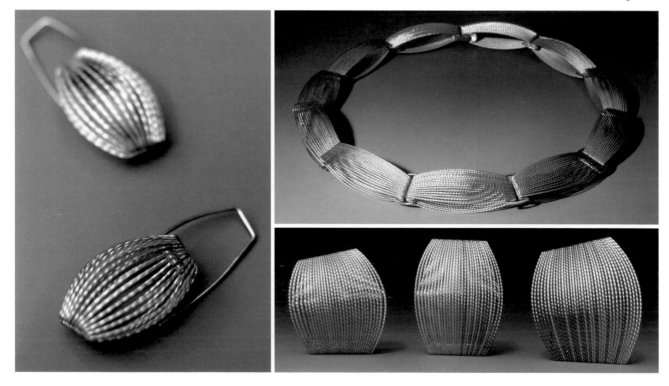

Sue Lane

My range of jewellery and one-off small-scale objects combine silver and gold to create work which has delicate and subtle qualities. The surface is given a soft matt finish to emphasise the subtle contrasts. My one-off objects incorporate wearable pieces of jewellery within a small sculpture. The viewer has to interact with the piece to discover the wearable element. The function being not immediately obvious results in intrigue, which I strive to achieve. The objects are intended to be a 'home' to the jewellery, offering it value and importance off the body as well as on.

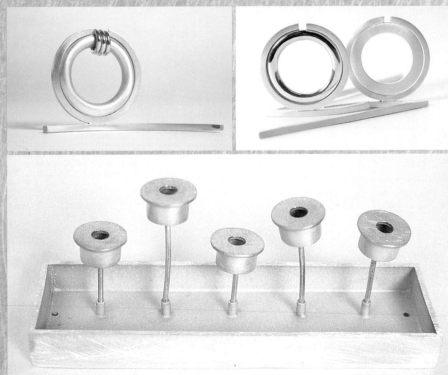

Holding, Ring and Holder – silver, 9ct gold

Two Halves Make, Ring and Holder – silver, 9ct gold

One Pair Plus 3, Earrings and Holder – silver, 9ct gold

Jo Lavelle

My work is characterised by using small components to create a sculptural and kinetic feel. These components, which I call silver tags, are grouped together in varying quantities and added to rings, earrings, bangles and neckpieces. My latest work which I title 'Pompom' sees the tags grouped together in a round sculptural manner, which move and can be heard by the wearer.

40 Pompom Rings
– silver, cast units

20 Pompom Earrings
– silver, cast units

Carole Leonard

I am currently using perspex and silver to make jewellery for everyday wear. These materials allow me to combine colour and pattern within a simple outline shape, contrasting the tactile qualities of warm and cold materials against the body. Asymmetrical designs mean colour balance changes with movement, exploring the personal and the public perception of a piece of jewellery.

Bangles – silver, laminated perspex

JOËL DEGEN

Sarah Letts

Sarah Letts focuses on making one-off pieces, each with its own distinct identity and signature. Striated engraving enhances the colours and transparency of the enamel, bringing a unique depth and luminosity to the work. Gold and silver are polished to a satin finish, creating exciting tactile contrasts between metal and glass. Each work embodies a moment of light suspended in time.

Brooch – silver, 18ct gold, champlevé enamel

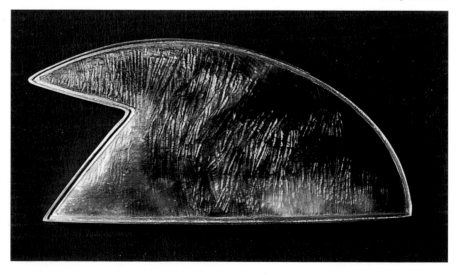

Anna Lewis

My current work is inspired by a body of research into the theme of memory and its importance in preserving personal identity and history. I use white feathers and soft leather that are printed with traces of imagery which evoke delicate, ghost-like qualities alluding to the fragile and transient nature of memory.

I interpret my ideas through a collection of jewellery and also larger one-off wearable art pieces. These pieces wrap around and embrace the neck and shoulders like a security blanket. The sensitivity and lightness of the feather contrasts with the idea that memory is often heavy with meaning.

Rings – silver, printed feathers
Layered Feather Neckpiece
– wire, crin, feathers

Meng-Jung Li

Tranquillity cocooned: The oldest textile material with the newest technique. Another dimension for silk making. Layering and wrapping objects inside to bring silk back to the original form of cocoon. Silk is luxury, refined, elegant, royal and heavenly. It is exotic and erotic. Most of all, it is simply sheer beauty.

Coming from an oriental country, looking for the right leaves to rear silk worms and observing its weaving was part of a science project in elementary school. Listening to the legend of the silk worm princess and admiring the autumn full moon is part of my tradition. In eastern society, being sharp or strong is not necessary. Harmony, consistency and persistence are important. I would like to think my silk pieces practise this ancient wisdom.

Leaf Bangle – felting, silk
Autumn Bangle – felting,
silk with alpaca hair

Tina Lilienthal

The two necklaces 'Gluttony' and 'Lust' are part of a series based on the seven deadly sins. Themes and stories play an important role in my work. The pieces relate to each other and can work in an installation, fashion or theatre context. I am interested in using materials that don't necessarily fit into conventional jewellery practice. Mixing for example shoelace, silver and silicon creates an exciting tension and expressiveness, making the pieces more universal.

Lust Necklace – silver, silicon, ribbon, casting

Gluttony Necklace – silver, silicon, ribbon, electroforming

73

Karen Lord

I like the sculptural possibilities of
jewellery design, although the
limitations of size often frustrate me.
My influences come from just about
everywhere: machinery, plants,
buildings, insects, books and
landscape. I am interested in the
way a metal surface develops
character as it is knocked,
scratched and worn with age. I
prefer this visible history to a static,
'perfect' and highly polished finish.

Swiss Army Ring
– silver, brass

JAN BLAKE

Anna Lorenz

I explore form, scale and material in relation to objects and jewellery. Through the use of geometric shapes, the circle and the square, ideas investigate structural compositions, which embrace space rather than enclose it. Most of the pieces are a result of working directly with materials in an intuitive way.

'Wear and ware' plays with shapes and moods, transformation and perception. Jewellery as object – object as jewellery.
I create pieces that allow the transition from a contemplative sculptural object to an interesting body adornment. Where to place 'wear and ware' – a decision that lies ultimately with the wearer.

Prickly Chain – silver, slate
Wear and Ware, Chain-Object-Chain – silver, stainless steel, slate

Jane Macintosh

My jewellery is individually made and is constructed out of simple classic shapes which can on occasion be used or distorted in unexpected ways. I combine different precious metals, working them together seamlessly which gives subtle contrasts of tone and colour, enhanced by a smooth, satin finish, and I sometimes add gemstones as highlights.

The directness and simplicity of Bauhaus design has been the most important influence on my work but also many artists including Barbara Hepworth and Constantin Brancusi.

Illusion Brooches – silver, 18ct gold

Joan MacKarell

I am an artist enamellist who designs and makes jewellery and smallwork using precious metals and semi-precious stones and beads. I feel that enamelling, the process of fusing glass to metal, is the means of using a rich and diverse medium to convey a personal response to ideas and visual experiences.

My childhood was spent in the North Atlantic Irish landscape of ancient rocks and wild seas.

Now that I live in London, my work is about trying to make sense of that history. It deals with the patina of time – the fragments revealed by the continual influence of the elements on surfaces and textures. The varied colours of the glass combined with textures and foils can produce a wonderfully tactile surface which is unlike any other material. Although enamel has inbuilt fragility, it is for me the perfect means of creating a lasting image.

Rock Necklace – jasper, copper and enamel beads

Homage to the Gecko, Collar – agate, silver and enamel beads

Susan May

My work is an exploration of abstract linear forms, inspired by observation of the natural world, musical sounds and the techniques and processes involved in making. By forging and manipulating silver and gold wires, my intention is to produce structures for the body which are both a visual and a sensual pleasure for the wearer.

Recollection Pendant – forged silver
Memento Pendant – forged silver
Bangle – forged silver

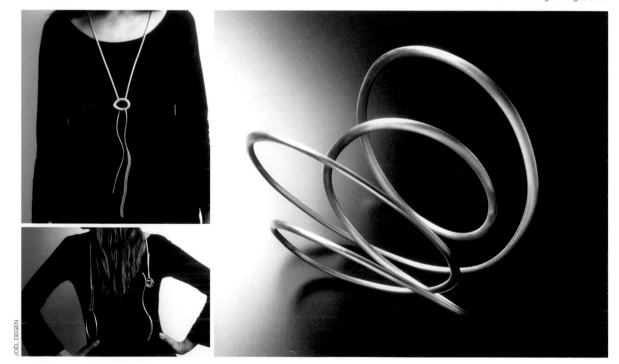

JOËL DEGEN

78

Barbie McClure

My designs evolve from abstract lines and shapes found both in weathered surfaces and architectural structures, and from exposed layers and edges revealed through erosion, evoking a sense of history. Using steel in different ways, in combination with silver, gives contrast and tension between surface texture and strength of materials.

Neckpieces – silver, steel

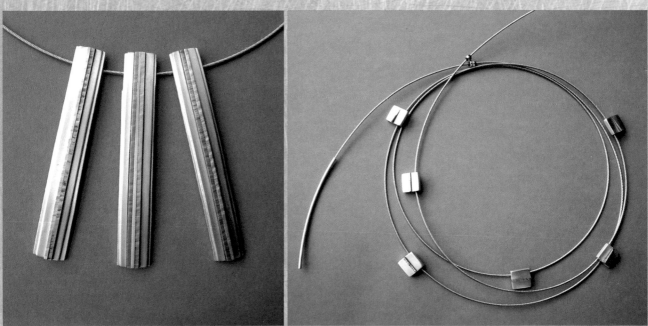

JAN BLAKE

Louise Miller

Cutting techniques are central to my theme of work and combine both hand and laser cutting. The nature of hand cutting also alludes to the popular belief of jewellery making being a time-consuming undertaking.

For me, the act of making is of equal importance as the end product and I aim to make contemporary objects that play on notions of traditional craft skills.

The forms take their starting point in jewellery but have applications beyond this. Wearable pieces might become objects that exist independently from the body, showing how similar structures can have more than one purpose.

Eye Bracelets
– laser cut polypropylene

Expanding Bracelets
– laser cut polypropylene

Jacqueline Mina

In my work I aim to achieve an aesthetic result that obscures the technical rigours of its production. I am preoccupied mainly with the surfaces of precious metals (which I always affect in some way before construction begins) and with form – juxtaposing the play of light, reflection, lustre with characteristic angle, curve and line – inspired by an abstraction of nature and art, and particularly of the human form. I am intrigued, too, by the potential for dialogue between inner and outer planes, with random patterns imprisoned within strictly delineated edges and the visual tension created by the contrast and harmony of all these factors.

Earrings – platinum, fine gold, diamonds
Necklace – platinum, fine gold

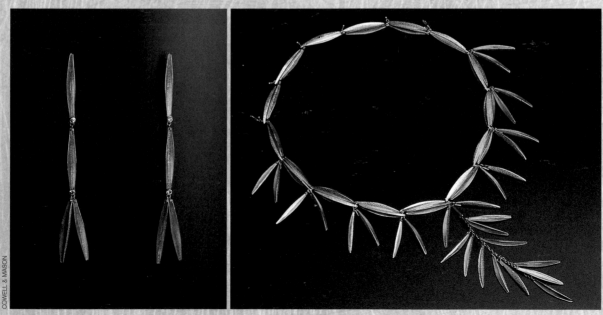

COWELL & MASON

81

Xavier Ines Monclús

Jewellery to play or toys to wear? Xavier Ines Monclús flirts with this ambiguity when he brings his jewellery to the limits of wearability. Inspired by the everyday life and the careful appropriation of pictures and objects from the childhood world, he has created a ludic universe inhabited by strange inventions, senseless machines of Dadaist echoes, and hybrids from animals and architecture. Arising from accumulation and eclecticism these pieces, basically brooches, appear like a collage of printed images. The frequent surrealistic associations give both a poetic and ironic charge to this work, whose open interpretation asks for a reflection by the observer.

Life's Long Baby, Brooch – silver, wood, plastic, plastificated paper

Brutality, Brooch – silver, plastic, plastificated paper, enamel paint

Jane Moore

This collection of jewellery is based on geometric and abstract forms. Jane plays with shapes within shapes creating small areas of transparent enamels that appear jewel-like in the brushed silver. She uses photo-etching to give a crisp and concise effect.

Colour is actually the most important aspect of her work and she has found transparent enamel to be her perfect medium.
Even though a very difficult process, Jane enjoys the ongoing challenge of applying glass to silver achieving a clean quality.

Target Pendant
– silver, enamel

Circle Brooch and Pendant
– silver, enamel

Strawberry Seed Pendant
– silver, enamel

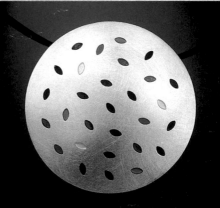

Anne Morgan

Anne enjoys silver's potential for texture and her ranges explore the relationship of look and feel in the materials she uses. Her creations proudly show off their origins in workshop experimentation.
She forges a relationship between organic texture and a simple geometry, rather like the placing of a formal structure in a natural landscape. She sets up a coupling in which each element complements the other. The results include objects that express a tactile sensuality, a dreamy sense of security, or even absentminded playfulness.

*Multidomed Necklace
– reticulated silver*

Roger Morris

The work shown highlights the development of a unique method of setting gemstones. The technique involves the accurate clamping of the stones using rivets to secure the setting and where appropriate allows more of the stone to be exposed. The cut of the stones used in the rings have strongly influenced the designs, although in the larger pieces the design theme leads and the setting principle has been adapted.

Although contemporary in design there are strong influences from research into past cultures, especially that of Ancient Egypt as well as the pre-Columbian period.

Ring – 18ct gold, tourmaline
Ring – 18ct gold, peridot

Kathie Murphy

I make jewellery using polyester resin. This is a thermosetting plastic that starts in liquid form. A catalyst is added to the liquid and this triggers a chemical reaction which polymerises the plastic to a solid. I have been using this material for the last ten years. As I have worked with resin, ideas for further pieces come from a mixture of working directly with the material, understanding its properties and less so by external influences that inspire me.

I have always been interested in using colour and non-precious materials in jewellery. The jewellery I make is a result of exploring the material and combining light, colour and shape to produce pieces that are wearable and tactile.

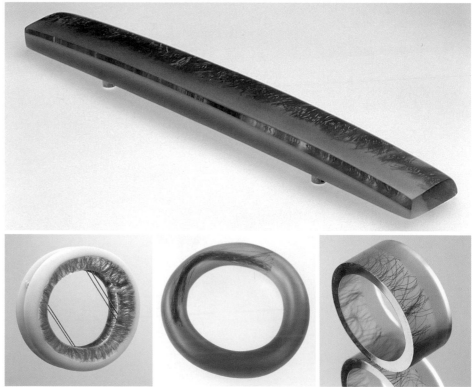

Bangles – polyester resin, thread
Brooches – polyester resin, thread

NORMAN HOLLANDS

Gill Newton

I have a strong belief in truth to materials and usually leave my pieces unpolished with subtle surface textures to emphasise the innate qualities of the metal. Natural lines and forms and their relationship to the body inspire all my pieces. I strive to evoke a sense of strength and confidence through the simplicity of line and use of form and texture. I use traditional jewellery techniques, often leaving a trace of hammer marks to distinguish my work from mass manufacture. Ultimately I want my work to be worn, touched and enjoyed.

Ovals Neckpiece
– silver, 9ct gold

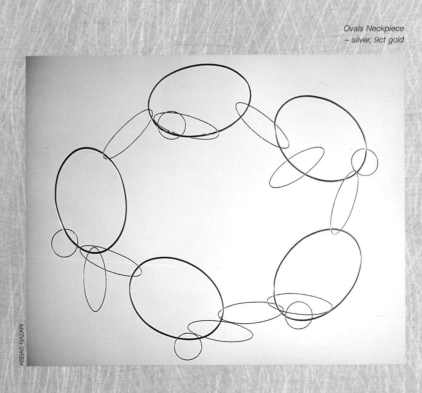

ABBAS NAZARI

87

Syann van Niftrik

My work draws freely from the
environment without being
representational. The techniques I
use are simple, relying on form and
tactile appeal. Most pieces are
hammer formed, some simply
relying on form, others made up of
repeated pieces linked in such a
way as to give maximum
movement.

*Leaffall Bracelet
– silver, planished and linked*

*Kintoo Necklace – oxidised
silver, planished and linked*

Simone Nolden

"Thus the task is not so much to see what one has not yet seen, but to think differently about that which everybody sees"

Arthur Schopenhauer.

Discovering things in unlikely settings is the main inspiration behind my work. Exploring the past history of everyday objects, reshaping them and ultimately altering their purpose, impels people to think differently about their use.

Necklace – silver, copper, enamel, heads, slate, found objects

Necklace – silver, copper, enamel, slate, glass beads, found objects

Jewellery for Wounds – plasters and synthetic gems

Mark Nuell

Mark Nuell has always placed great importance on vividly coloured gemstones. As a child he lived on the Australian gemfields and collected tiny, brightly coloured chips of sapphires. This initial interest in gems led him to study at the Randwick College in Sydney.

Mark carefully selects stones for their colour, luminosity and brilliance, setting them in silver and 22ct gold.

His spiral rings and bangles are hand-forged, with fancy coloured sapphires and diamonds set playfully on the surface. The simplicity of form belies the complexity of his jewellery and illustrates successfully the very demanding techniques of jewellery making and stone setting.

Neckpiece – silver, 18ct gold, diamonds

Ring – forged silver with yellow sapphire

Ulli Oberlack

These objects are the first from 'i+e illumination and emotion: light as body adornment', the research project I have been working on at Central St Martins College of Art and Design, London.

Rapid developments in lighting technologies have opened exciting new possibilities for working with light on the body, allowing objects that redefine the boundaries of jewellery. My vision is to exploit the intrinsic characteristics of light on the body creating new forms of adornment. I intend to develop my research to make pieces that range from theatrical and totally experimental to simple practical objects.

Feuerrad – silver, LEDs, fibre optic cable, customised electronics

Travelling Light – aluminium, LEDs, customised electronics

Sous Vetements – aluminium, LEDs, customised electronics

Hiroko Okuzawa

Wrap Up Collection: I am always interested in the relationship between jewellery and the body. I am also interested in modern architecture, its dynamic relation with nature and the human body. The inner shape of these pieces dramatises the surface of the body and echoes its curves, while the hardness of the surface and the use of materials such as steel and plastic creates a contrast to the softness and smoothness of the body. As architecture creates boundaries between inner and outer space, my pieces also have this dichotomy; the inside suggests a personal space while the outside indicates a more anonymous face.

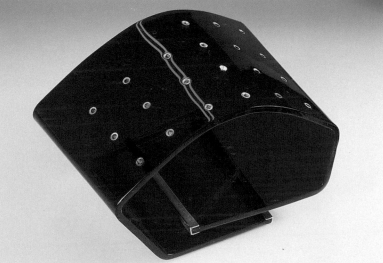

Rings – silver, perspex
Bangle – silver, perspex

Nina Osborne

This collection came about after spending time reflecting on society's tastes and acceptance levels, and their constantly shifting boundaries. More specifically, the work became about my own shifting boundaries and aesthetic ideals. For a long time I had rejected tradition and a modernist aesthetic was my inspiration, but while I was looking to pure form, tradition also began to have its appeal.

An investigative approach has resulted in a body of work which explores the inherited identities of both 'modern' and 'traditional' aesthetics, as well as considering how they fit into personal ideals and memories, and my developing affection for traditional pattern.

Egg and Cube Neckpiece
– silver, resin, chickens egg, steel
Orange Brooch – silver, resin, steel
Yellow Brooch – silver, resin, steel

Adam Paxon

Taking influence from nature's colourful language of warning and courtship I make mainly one-off pieces of acrylic jewellery. Although diverse, I find acrylic's stock colours too insensitive, but processes of lamination forming and carving allow the blending of colours and remove the material from its industrial/mass produced context. I'm fascinated by the way pieces can be fixed to clothing or worn on the body and seek new and unusual approaches to wearability. I am also interested in pieces' value as objects in their own right. I try to give them a dual identity and often see them as 'creatures to wear'.

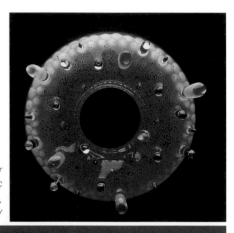

Brooch – acrylic, lacquer
Rings with Tails – acrylic, PVC
Squirming Brooches – acrylic, lamination, carving, inlay

Diana Porter

Inspiration is drawn from the personal and political beliefs I have developed through my life experience. Words are a major feature of the work – they are used as decoration and may be ambiguous in their meaning, often words are split between two, three or four pieces so that the marks on an individual ring are indecipherable until put together with another piece. The work is perhaps best known for the words 'on and on'.

The collection is made in the Bristol workshop by a team of jewellers and I design and make one-off commissions in gold, platinum and silver.

Stacking Rings
– silver, 22ct gold

Square Bead Necklace
– silver, fine gold

Suzanne Potter

This group of work is connected thematically by the 'senses'. They celebrate touch, sight and sound. For me, the senses are about enquiry and discovery. Each piece holds its own secret, which is only discovered when handled/worn, therefore revealing its purpose and concept.

Bubble Blower, Plaything – silver

Touchzone Brooch
– white metal, stainless steel

Holding Noise # 3, 4 Rings
– silver, steel shot

Pamela Rawnsley

Throughout my work, strong clear forms are combined with subtly textured and coloured surfaces. Much of my jewellery is of hollow construction, light to wear, and may be used or worn in several ways.

A box forms the display base for this set of pins. Each are objects in their own right, and are also wearable. I like to blur the distinction between work to be worn and work to be used.

Four Pins – silver

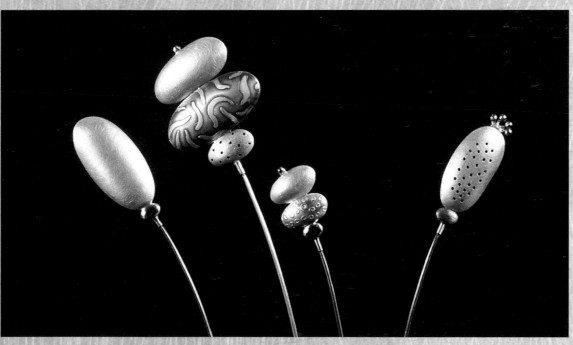

Melissa Rigby

Many of my designs evolve from experimenting and playing with materials. I like to push boundaries and use materials in unconventional ways. I also like to produce interactive jewellery which can be played with. The bangles explore the way close cuts in flat sheet enable the material to be flexed or pulled out in different ways with new forms held by tension. I also love to use colour and to explore the subtle hues of transparent enamels and their wonderful reflective quality.

Green Bangle
– silver, polypropylene

Tamizan Savill

Colour is central to my work.
The clarity of transparent enamel
merits the demands of working with
this versatile material. Watching a
fired piece cool from red hot
through various colour changes to
its final state has an almost
alchemical feel, like watching a
photograph develop.

JOEL DEGEN

Brooch – silver, enamel

Jean Scott-Moncrieff

Large hollow geometric forms –
elegantly wearable whilst having a
strong visual impact.
The surface of the silver is fused with
high-carat golds, then hammered or
impressed with subtle textures and
hand finished to leave a matt
surface. My work is influenced by
ancient and tribal artefacts.

*Bangle – hollow silver
with fused 18ct gold*

*Bangle – hollow silver
with oxidised surface*

PETER WHYTE

Vannetta Seecharran

Fashion and textiles are the main inspirations for my work. Metal serves as the main structure for the piece and fabrics offer the tactile quality. Wearable objects are a consistent and central theme throughout my work. In my current work I seek to create a dialogue between the two materials so that neither is dominant but instead can work harmoniously. In this way the piece functions on two levels – as jewellery and as art.

Bracelets – silver, ribbons, fabric

Dot Sim

My designs are inspired by my environment – starry skies, changing landscapes, the sea. I use photography to capture visual stimulation, and then 'draw' with the metal to create dramatic but wearable jewellery. I choose to use precious metals – materials that will stand the test of time – as I am interested in the role of jewellery as heirlooms that are handed down, providing intimate memories for future generations.

Wave Neckpiece – forged silver
Roller Bangle – forged silver

Scilla Speet

As jewellery designer/maker I am often invited to work beside other researchers who are developing new alloys/new materials. In the case of design work currently being developed my collaborative work with Dr Geesin (researcher in industrial/ smart materials and fabrics) started just over two years ago. The creative dynamic between us enables us to explore design possibilities and limitations in context of the material, its beauty and researched techniques which maximise our application of skills and knowledge.

Leaf Neckpiece – silver, aluminium leaves using PVD process

Leaf Earrings – silver, aluminium leaves using PVD process

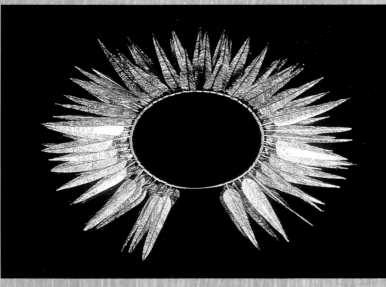

DONOVAN BAXENDALE

103

Bettina Starke

Strong, simple shapes with functional details incorporated into the overall design. Preferred materials are silver in conjunction with high grade gold alloys as well as stones, ranging from precious to road aggregate. Techniques include sheet construction and casting. Surface treatments involve predominantly abrasion processes as well as oxidising and gilding.

Necklace
– german lava, silver

Necklace
– sponge coral, silver

Stephanie Summerhill

The jewellery that I make is designed as an accessory, either to enhance the wearer's outfit or to be worn and simply enjoyed. Using a combination of materials such as resin and anodised aluminium to provide bold colours, together with acrylic for its transparency and silver for brightness and strength, my jewellery contains detail and intrigue.

Simple, crisp, precise shapes in a range of different designs are created through a variety of production methods and up to date technology – such as laser marking techniques. I gain inspiration from a wide variety of sources, particularly things relating to 60s and 70s design, especially pattern and shape which I am drawn to because of their simplicity.

Finger Rings – cast resin

Lucy Jade Sylvester

I'm motivated by using unpopular insects. If a ladybird landed on a woman's knee she would probably accept it, however if a cockroach walked up her leg it would not be welcome. I find the thought of creating jewellery that will be worn close to the skin, from a mould taken directly from the insects she would loathe to be near, fascinating. I'm drawn to preserving the insects delicate forms, saving them from the effects of time, also the twisted pleasure of a woman being adorned by the insect she would no doubt swat in everyday life.

I have explored how entomologists and museums store and file their collections. I like how each item has a history, where it was found, the date and who found it.

I decided to document every insect used in my work, each piece of jewellery is labelled with the history of the insect it was formed from.

Fly and Poppy Head
Cufflinks – silver

Moth and Poppy Head
Ring – silver

Jessica Turrell

My current body of work is part of a formal investigation into mark making and pattern, using large-scale enamel techniques not traditionally associated with jewellery. This group of pieces stem from a period of technical research and exploration. They are enamelled using etching, drawing and sifting techniques.
I am interested in creating pieces where the enamelled surface is not immediately identifiable as such.
I avoid using enamel for its colour and shine and instead choose to work with a monochromatic palette and to etch and abrade the surface to achieve a pebble-like tactile finish.

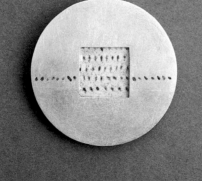

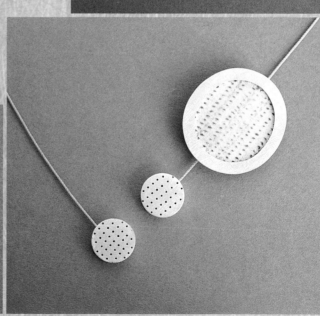

Winter # 1, 2 Brooches
– silver, enamel
Winter # 3 Brooch
– silver, enamel
Winter Neckpiece
– silver, enamel

Clara Vichi

In my jewellery making, predominantly the brooch, I use calligraphy and typography as my inspiration to form wearable pieces. I isolate parts of letter forms or sections of sentences and in doing so draw the eye to the line width and form, curve and delineation so the beauty of a letter is given new prominence. I also paint wood for colour, depth and texture complementary to the letter forms.

Calligraphic Brooch
– etched and oxidised silver, brass

Jenny Walker

My work revolves around the desire to incorporate non-precious found objects into wearables. Through the use of items which hold personal significance, I explore jewellery types and consider notions of precious content and issues of wearability. I am fascinated by discards and attitudes to consumables in our 'throw-away' culture and often compare past and present values concerning the useful lives of objects. My current work uses fragments of Victorian pottery, some collected in childhood, others gathered more recently from my urban environment in Manchester. All hold memories of their discovery and intrigue as to what the complete object may once have been.

Pendant – silver, found object

Frances Julie Whitelaw

Whatever medium I work in, I try to exploit the potential of that material and to use this to direct my design ideas.

Three-dimensional form is also an important factor in the development of a piece of jewellery, as is its tactile quality. How it feels to the touch and how it feels to wear are part of design from first ideas to finished object.

Brooch – 18ct gold wire
Earrings – 18ct gold wire
Pendant – silver wire

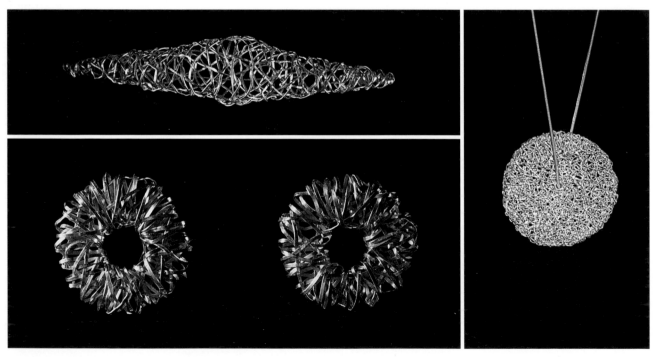

Sandra Wilson

I'm interested in the basic organic principles underpinning our genetics – the relationships and systems that exist in the ways in which our genes make the human form. I believe that by examining how our DNA connects and how proteins are formed, for example, provides innovative and creative forms of jewellery and ways of wearing. As a conceptual jeweller exploring the interface between craft and science, my work also goes further in asking – what can the scientist learn from the craft person's holistic processes of making and creation?

Protein Strands
– 3 strands, fine silver wire,
natural permanent magnets

Earrings – silver

Anthony Wong

Wave shows the results of my initial exploration into the concepts of jewellery as sculpture, an ornamental piece, or as a statement of the maker and the wearer. Wave is unashamedly sculptural in form, and so... imagine yourself sliding down the pinkie ring, hiding in the curve of the bangle, making faces in the hugely curved mirror or falling asleep in the hammock of the pendant... smiling.

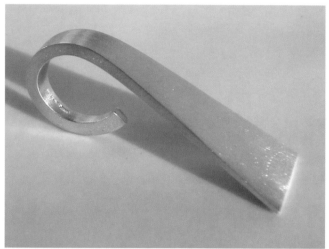

Wave! Pinkie Ring
– forged & filed silver

Wave! Index Ring
– forged & filed silver

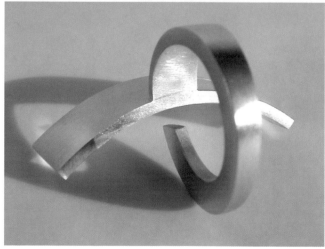

Galleries where contemporary jewellery can be seen, bought and commissioned

3D Gallery
13 Perry Road, Bristol BS1 5BG
Phone: 0117 929 1363
e-mail: anny@gallery3d.demon.co.uk

The Architecture Centre
Narrow Quay, Bristol BS1 4QA
Phone: 0117 922 1540
e-mail: shop@architecturecentre.co.uk
website: www.arch-centre.demon.co.uk

Black Swan Arts
2 Bridge Street, Frome, Somerset BA11 1BB
Phone: 01373 473 980
e-mail: ann@blackswan.org.uk
website: www.blackswan.org.uk

Bluecoat Display Centre
Bluecoat Chambers, School Lane, Liverpool L1 3BX
Phone: 0151 709 4014
e-mail: crafts@bluecoatdisplaycentre.com
website: www.bluecoatdisplaycentre.com

Church House Designs
Broad Street, Congresbury, Bristol BS49 5DG
Phone: 01934 833 660
website: www.churchhousedesigns.co.uk

Collections of Harpenden
The Leys, 38 High Street, Harpenden,
Hertfordshire AL5 2SX
Phone: 01582 620 015
e-mail: prcollections@aol.com
website: www.collectionsofharpenden.co.uk

Contemporary Applied Arts
2 Percy Street, London WIT 1DD
Phone: 020 7436 2344
website: www.caa.org.uk

The Craft Centre and Design Gallery
City Art Gallery, The Headrow, Leeds LS1 3AB
Phone: 0113 247 8241
e-mail: ccdg-art-leeds@pop3.poptel.org.uk
website: craftcentreleeds.co.uk

Dazzle Exhibitions
Old Farm Cottage, Frittenden, Cranbrook,
Kent TN17 2BE
Phone: 01580 852 503
e-mail: tonydazzle@aol.com
website: www.zone-d.com

Derek Topp Gallery
Chatsworth Road, Rowsley, Matlock,
Derbyshire DE4 2EH
Phone: 01629 735 580
e-mail: info@derektoppgallery.com
website: www.derektoppgallery.com

Designs Gallery
179 King Street, Castle Douglas, Scotland DG7 1DZ
Phone: 01556 504 552
e-mail: shop@designsgallery.co.uk
website: www.designsgallery.co.uk

Diana Porter Contemporary Jewellery
20 Cotham Hill, Bristol BS6 6LF
Phone: 0117 373 1025
e-mail: enquiries@dianaporter.co.uk
website: www.dianaporter.co.uk

Electrum Gallery
21 South Molton Street, London W1K 5QZ
Phone: 020 7629 6325

Ginger Gallery
84 – 86 Hotwell Road, Clifton, Bristol BS8 4UB
Phone: 0117 929 2527
website: www.gingergallery.co.uk

Godfrey and Watt
7 – 8 Westminster Arcade, Parliament Street,
Harrogate, North Yorkshire HG1 2RN
Phone: 01423 525 300
e-mail: mail@godfreyandwatt.co.uk
website: www.godfreyandwatt.co.uk

Imago
22 Fairfax Place, Dartmouth, Devon TQ6 9AB
Phone: 01803 835 105
e-mail: sarah.imago@btopenworld.com

Jane Moore Contemporary Jewellery
16 Denby Buildings, Regent Grove,
Leamington Spa, Warwickshire CV32 4NY
Phone: 01926 332 454
e-mail: jane@janemoore.co.uk
website: www.janemoorejewellery.co.uk

Kath Libbert Jewellery Gallery
The Store, 2nd floor, Salts Mill, Saltaire,
Bradford BD18 3LB
Phone: 01274 599 790
e-mail: kath.libbert@ukgateway.net
website: www.saltsmill.org.uk

Lesley Craze Gallery
33-35a Clerkenwell Green, London EC1R ODU
Phone: 020 7608 0393
e-mail: gallery@lesleycraze.demon.co.uk
website: www.lesleycrazegallery.co.uk

Made
Clifton Arcade, 1A Boyces Avenue,Clifton Village,
Bristol BS8 4AA
Phone: 0117 973 9448
e-mail: sarahjamesmade@aol.com

Manchester Craft and Design Centre
17 Oak Street, Manchester M4 5JD
Phone: 0161 832 4274
e-mail: manager@craftanddesign.com
website: www.craftanddesign.com

Mission Gallery
Gloucester Place, Maritime Quarter, Swansea SA1 1TY
Phone: 01792 652 016

New Ashgate Gallery
Wagon Yard, Farnham, Surrey GU9 7PS
Phone: 01252 713 208
e-mail: gallery@newashgate.org.uk
website: www.newashgategallery.com

OCG Jewellery
Market Place, Ambleside, Cumbria LA22 9BU
Phone: 015394 32022
e-mail: sylvia@ocg-arts.com
website: www.ocg-arts.com

St. James's Gallery
9b Margarets Buildings, Bath BA1 2LP
Phone: 01225 319 197
website: www.bathshopping.co.uk

The Scottish Gallery
16 Dundas Street, Edinburgh EH3 6HZ
Phone: 0131 558 1200
e-mail: mail@scottish-gallery.co.uk
website: www.scottish-gallery.co.uk

Studio Fusion Gallery
Unit 1:06, Oxo Tower Wharf, Bargehouse Street,
South Bank, London SE1 9PH
Phone: 020 7928 3600
e-mail: info@studiofusiongallery.co.uk
website: www.studiofusiongallery.co.uk

Turning Heads
52 Meeting House Lane, Brighton BN1 1HB
Phone: 01273 772 645
e-mail: annie@turning-heads.net
website: www.turning-heads.net

UNO Gallery
5 South Street, Chesterfield S40 1QX
Phone: 01246 557 145

Wave Contemporary Jewellery
37 Market Place, Kendal, Cumbria LA9 4TP
Phone: 01539 729 805
2 Ash Street, Bowness-on-Windermere,
Cumbria LA23 2EB
Phone: 015394 48022
27 Marketgate, Lancaster, Lancashire LA1 1AL
Phone: 01524 62333
e-mail: info@wavejewellery.co.uk
website: www.wavejewellery.co.uk

Acknowledgements

Grateful thanks are due to the following for their help and support:

Jane Adam, Uschi Arens-Price, Pepe Argo, Jivan Astfalck-Prall, Kathleen Bailey, Helen Bawden, BCT Aviation. Kemble, Elizabeth Bell, J. Blundell and Sons Ltd, Johanna Bolhoven, Sarah Braun, Ted Braun, Sarah Jane Bright, Tony Cowley at Bristol Guild of Applied Arts, Lilian Busch, Bristol School of Art, Matt Chelmicki, Norman Cherry, Lin Cheung, Hanne Christensen, Anne-Marie Craig, A J Cutler, Joël Degen, Lila Diamantopoulou, Amanda Doughty, Ruth Facey, George Ferguson, Gail Ferriman, Gill Forsbrook, Susan Fortune, Roi Gal-Or, Lady Gibberd, Dennis Teeth, Shelby Fitzpatrick, Elizabeth Goring, Madeleine Grove, Annette Guck at 3-D Gallery, Colin and Nicky Harper, Collette Hazelwood, Harold Hedges at Dragon Workshop, Fionna Hesketh, Dorothy Hogg,

Tessa Holland, Sue Hollingsworth, Geraldine Hollweg, Beata Høst, Philip Hughes, Vivica and Tony Hunter, Jill Hutchings, Sue Hyams, Inspirals.co.uk, Rachel Kerrison, Marcia Lanyon Ltd, Anna Lewis, Carole Lockwood, Karen & Peter Lord, Caroline Lytton, Mary Macdonald, Bristol Magpies, Majestic Wines, Ian Major, Gill Mallett, Carol Marks, Hannah Martin, Rodger Martin, Barbie & Tim McClure, Nicky & Mike McNamara, Lisa Cains at The Mid-Cornwall School of Jewellery, Tom Miles, Deborah Miller, Lynn Miller, Jacqueline Mina, Jane Moore, Roger Morris, Ronald Murray, Maria Neath, Gill Newton, Syann Van Niftrik, Nunn Rossiter castings Ltd, Julia Palmer, Pam Parker, Samantha Parks, Matthew Partington, Hazel Passmore, Michael Peckitt, Steve Perring, Diana Porter,

Potters (London) Ltd, Jeremy Prosser, Andy Purnell, Keith Reay, Annabel Rees, Kathy Reeves, John Rogers, Janet Roome, Jean Scott Moncrieff, Veronica Shaw, Saskia Shutt, Rosemary Silvester, Mark Simmons, Heather Skowood, Paula Spielman, Harriet St Leger, Philip Stanley, Erica Steer of Arts Council England, Gillian Stein, Lila Stern-Shewry, Sarah Stewart, tableau displays, James Taljaard at Arts and Business SW, Caroline Tetley, Thomson Directories, Jacqueline Tierney, The Tobacco Factory, Elizabeth Turrell, Roger Turrell, UWE, Carole Waller, Karin Walton & staff at Bristol City Museums & Art Gallery, Jeanne Werge-Hartley, Katie White, Basement Gallery, Muriel Wilson, Kate Wright at The Architecture Centre, Heidi Yeo, Deborah Zeldin-O'Neill, and Waitrose.